SNOWBLIND

For Joseph and Anna

SNOWBLIND

Paul Stewart

Illustrated by Chris Molan

OXFORD
UNIVERSITY PRESS

Contents

CHAPTER 1

Out of the blue

'Hang onto your hats back there,' called the pilot. 'We're coming in for landing, and I'm afraid it's going to be a bumpy one.'

Meg groaned. The little six-seater plane had been bouncing around for the past hour. Now it was going to get worse. To take her mind off the turbulence, she closed her eyes and went over the chain of events that had brought her to the snowy wasteland they were flying over.

Last Tuesday her dad had arrived home with news of his latest assignment. It was a trip north to Bolam Island – a vast, mountainous island which straddled the Arctic Circle – to film the way of life of the local Inuit people for a TV documentary series called *This World*.

'I leave next Monday,' her dad had announced.

'What about me?' Meg asked. Her mum was on a sales-tour and wouldn't be back until the end of the following week.

'Well,' said her dad slowly. 'It *is* the holidays. You're thirteen now – and I could do with a research assistant.' He smiled. 'Would you like to come along?'

Meg's eyes widened. 'You bet!' she exclaimed. 'Oh, thanks, Dad. I won't be any trouble, I promise.'

Remembering that promise now, Meg opened her eyes and turned to her dad. She smiled bravely. 'It's better than a rollercoaster,' she said.

'That's my girl,' said her dad. 'It shouldn't be long now till . . . hey, look down there!'

Meg looked out of the window and gasped. They had broken through the thick white clouds at last. The view was breathtaking. To the left were glistening, snow-capped mountains with steep, dark cliff-faces; to the right, shadowed plains of snow stretched down towards the slate-grey sea, where the sun shone low on the horizon.

'It's amazing,' she whispered.

As the pilot banked to the left, the view changed. Hugging the coast of the bay below them was a cluster of matchbox houses.

'That must be downtown Prospect,' said her dad, and laughed. 'And look. There's the runway.'

'That little thing!' said Meg. The so-called runway looked absurdly short. It came closer. Meg made herself keep watching. Closer and closer and – *ker-dunk* – the wheels came down. The pilot brought the plane safely to a standstill and looked round.

'Welcome to Bolam Island,' he said.

Meg smiled to herself. She'd read books and seen videos about the place, she'd surfed the net for details. Now she was actually here. And all in one piece! Her Arctic adventure was about to begin.

CHAPTER 2

The top of the world

Meg's legs were still shaking as she made her way from the plane. The air outside was crisp and bitterly cold. It stung the inside of her nose and turned her breath to thick, billowing clouds. She zipped up her jacket.

There were two men waiting to greet them. One was young – about sixteen or seventeen, Meg guessed. The other was old. His face was heavily lined and his hair, once jet black, was now as white as the snow all round them.

'Hi,' said the younger one as the visitors stepped down onto the runway. 'This is my grandfather, Nanuk Palituk. My name's Joe.'

'Pleased to meet you both,' said Meg's dad. 'I'm Ted Sundberg. This is Ricky Travis, my cameraman and Donna Lewinson, my sounds engineer. And this,' he said, pushing Meg gently forwards, 'is Meg. My research assistant – and daughter.'

'Hello,' said Meg shyly.

The old man's eyes crinkled as he leaned forward to shake her hand. His skin felt dry and leathery. 'You are many miles from where you live,' he said. 'While you are here, may this too be your home.'

Meg smiled. 'Thanks,' she said.

'Right, then,' said Joe. 'Shall we be off? Ted and Meg are to stay with my grandparents. Ricky and Donna have got rooms above Prospect's one and only attraction – the Seal Cafe.'

'Sounds good to me,' said Ricky.

'So long as there's a bed, I'll be happy,' said Donna, yawning.

Meg realized that she, too, was tired. It had been a long day's travelling and, although the sun had still not set, it was almost midnight. She rubbed her itchy eyes.

'Come on, sleepy head,' said her dad. 'Let's get inside. We've got an early start tomorrow.'

With Nanuk leading the way, the three of them set off through the snow-packed streets. Although marked on the map, Prospect could hardly be called a town. It was a chaotic sprawl of clapboard houses and workshops. There was a general store with a post-room, the Seal Cafe, a small school . . .

Nanuk sighed. 'The national government means well,' he said. 'But their school teaches our children to want what they do not need. They learn many things, but forget how to live in their own land. I fear that they will never be able to return to the old way of life.'

Meg looked up at her father. He was nodding sympathetically. 'That's why I'm here, Nanuk,' he said. 'To record your way of life. To learn from it. To preserve those survival techniques which have been passed down over the centuries, from generation to generation, and ensure they *don't* get lost.'

Nanuk smiled sadly. 'You are a good man, Ted

Sundberg,' he said, and patted him on the arm. 'Come, we are almost there.'

Meg hung back as they continued walking. For the first time ever, she felt embarrassed by her dad. She knew he meant well, but all that talk of 'recording' and 'preserving' made it sound as though he was putting something in a museum, not making a programme about living people.

Nanuk pointed ahead. 'My house,' he said.

With its sloping roof and shuttered windows, it looked like all the rest. A thin twist of smoke escaped from a tin chimney and veered off sharply to the right. It made Meg realize how windy it had become – and how much colder. The icy blast was slicing through her padded jacket like a knife. Fine, dry flakes of snow writhed along the road.

If it's this cold in August, she thought, what on earth is it like in January?

Nanuk noticed her shiver. 'You need a caribou-skin parka,' he said. 'We have spares.'

'Thanks,' said Meg, uncertainly. She'd never liked the idea of wearing animal skins. Yet, here was Nanuk, standing before her, dressed in caribou skin from the top of his fur-edged hood to the tip of his lace-up boots.

'Very warm,' said Nanuk and continued walking.

Ted Sundberg had seen his daughter's face. 'The Inuit people depend on caribou, Meg,' he explained. 'And on walruses and seals. Every part of the animal they hunt is used. The meat for food. The fat for lighting, heating, cooking. The bones for spears and harpoons. The pelts for clothing . . .'

'You're right,' said Meg. 'And I'm sorry I . . .'

'Don't be sorry,' said her dad. 'It's useful to

know what you're thinking. Your reactions will be the reactions of the viewers. I've got to make it clear that the Inuit don't exploit their environment. They co-exist within it.'

Nanuk was climbing the snow-covered wooden steps to the front door. They hurried after him.

'Meg and Ted,' Nanuk said as they caught up. 'Welcome to our home!'

He opened the door and the three of them stepped inside. A woman was standing next to a stove at the far side of the room, frying fish in a pan. She turned, smiled shyly and greeted them in her own language.

'My wife, Kitty,' said Nanuk. 'Apart from the odd word of English and French, she speaks only Inupiaq. One of the last,' he added.

Kitty said something, her voice high pitched and staccato. 'Supper is ready,' Nanuk translated. 'Please, sit down.'

Meg unzipped her jacket, but then thought better of taking it off. The house was far from warm. She sat on one of the benches and looked round.

The whole place was a curious mish-mash of the old and the new. A plastic bowl and a thermos flask stood next to a handful of traditional utensils. A bare electric bulb shone in the middle of the room – yet there was a row of oil lamps on a shelf for those times when the central generator failed. And though supper was served on modern plates, the knives and spoons that Kitty handed them were made of beautifully carved bone.

Meg had already decided that she wouldn't complain, no matter what the meal was like. She was in an Inuit settlement, eating Inuit food. It would be unforgivably rude to turn anything down. Thankfully, the fried fish was delicious. There was also a piece of flat bread and a dark green vegetable that tasted like a cross between cabbage and asparagus.

'Good to see you eating your greens,' her dad laughed.

'Do you know what it is?' Meg asked.

'Seaweed of some sort, at a guess,' he said.

Meg nodded and took another mouthful.

By the time she had finished Meg was feeling

warm and contented. And while Nanuk and her dad pored over maps, droning on and on about where to go, her eyelids grew heavy.

'Bed, now,' said Kitty Palituk, smiling kindly down at her.

Meg climbed to her feet.

'Night-night, Meg,' said her dad.

'N'night,' Meg muttered sleepily. She allowed herself to be led into a small room where she lay down on the bed fully dressed, and was asleep before Kitty had even pulled the caribou-skin cover over her.

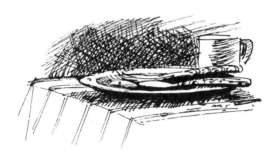

CHAPTER 3

Northern lights

Meg slept well. The bed cover kept her warm and snug, and her dreams were filled with mountains and snow and polar bears and . . .

Suddenly, she was wakened by a bright, flickering light. Her eyes snapped open. She sat up and stared out of the window. It was as though the whole sky was ablaze.

'The northern lights,' she breathed.

Meg had always longed to see the northern lights, or *aurora borealis*. She lived too far south to see it at home, but here, on top of the world, the lights were at their very best.

Scarcely daring to blink in case they disappeared, Meg went to the window. There was a huge glowing arch of red and turquoise spanning the sky, and shimmering curtains, streamers and ribbons of every possible shade and hue. Pinks and oranges, yellows, greens . . .

As if hypnotized, Meg ran back through the room, out of the back door – grabbing one of the caribou parkas from a hook as she went – and climbed up the rocky outcrop behind the house. At the top, she sat down and gazed ahead of her. The magnificent performance of lights continued, a thousand times better than any firework display.

'Pretty impressive, eh?' came a voice.

Meg spun round. 'Joe!' she said.

He hunkered down next to her. 'I always come up here when the lights are giving a show. Are these the first you've seen?'

Meg nodded.

'Come with me, then,' he said. 'I know an even better place to watch them. Quickly. Before they start to fade.'

The pair of them ran down the frozen scree-strewn slope on the far side of the hill and across the snowy plain. All the while, the curtains of light rippled across the sky in front of them.

'Nearly there,' Joe panted and, pointing towards a low wedge-shaped rock, ran on ahead.

Meg took a deep breath and hurried after him. The next moment, she heard something that made her blood run cold. She froze to the spot, cocked her head to one side and listened.

There it was again – far away in the distance, yet carried in on the wind – a faint, trumpeting howl, so plaintive that it made Meg want to weep.

'What was that?' she called to Joe, but her voice was whipped away on the wind.

She set off once again. But when she arrived at the rock, Joe had disappeared round the other side. She followed him, picking her way clumsily over the stony rubble – then looked up. All thought of the strange cry went from her mind.

'*Wow*!' she gasped.

'Told you!' said Joe triumphantly. 'It's called Gillie's Hollow. In summer, water lies on the surface like a giant lake. It's only a few centimetres deep. But when it freezes, it's like a mirror.'

'It's amazing,' Meg whispered.

The aurora was no longer in the sky alone. Reflected in the wide expanse of ice, it was as though the wonderful lights were shining right down into the centre of the Earth.

'Shall we go in,' Joe said, and he stepped forward onto the ice.

Meg followed, and burst out laughing. 'It's the most incredible thing I have ever, *ever* seen!' Above her, below her, the lights throbbed and pulsed; red and orange and ultraviolet blue. It was like dancing in the sky, like flying through a rainbow. It was magical.

When the display came to an end, however, it faded fast. The reflections dimmed and, by the time Meg and Joe got back to town, the aurora had all but disappeared. They stood behind Kitty and Nanuk's wooden house.

'Thanks for taking me,' said Meg.

'Glad you enjoyed it,' said Joe. 'I'll see you later. Grandad's arranged a seal-hunting trip for your dad to film, and he wants me to come along. He says I might learn something!' he added, and pulled a face. 'You wouldn't believe how *boring* seal hunting is!'

'But surely you need to know?' said Meg.

'Why?' said Joe. 'We get pizza and burgers flown in.'

'But . . .'

'Besides, I'm not going to stay in Prospect, Bolam Island. I want to go to a big city. New York or London. Tokyo. Toronto . . .' He kicked out at a lump of ice, sending it scudding away. 'This place might be OK for a holiday, but can you imagine living here?'

Meg shuffled her feet. She really didn't know what to say. In the end, it was Joe who broke the silence.

'There I go again,' he said. 'Sounding off. It's just . . . well, when you've heard about some-where exciting a long way off, you have to go and see it for yourself.'

Meg nodded. She knew *exactly* what Joe meant. She glanced at her watch. It was nearly three in the morning.

'I'd better get a bit more sleep,' she said. 'Thanks again for taking me to Gillie's Hollow.'

Joe nodded. 'Perhaps one day you'll show me something special where *you* live,' he said, and before Meg could answer, he had turned and gone.

CHAPTER 4

The old ways

Finally dressed to Kitty's satisfaction in the caribou-skin clothing, Meg joined the others outside and they all piled onto the two waiting snowmobiles. Ricky and Nanuk were on one; Donna, Meg and her dad, who was driving, on the other. Joe, for some reason, was not there – but Meg was too excited to be disappointed.

'All set?' her dad called out. A chorus of assent went up, and they were off. It was seven in the morning.

As they sped into the vast freezing landscape, Meg was left breathless. It was *so* beautiful.

Behind her the small town disappeared, while in front, far away in the distance, the mountain glaciers glistened in the cold rays of the sun. It was to this place, where winter never released its grip, that they were heading.

To her left, Meg saw a small group of caribou, cream and grey against the silvery snow. They paused and watched the passing snowmobiles – and Meg couldn't help feeling a twinge of guilt at the thought of what she was wearing.

On and on they went. Her dad kept to the tracks made by Nanuk's snowmobile. The old man knew where the ground was hard, and where it gave way to treacherous hollows. It was more than an hour later when they finally stopped. Meg climbed stiffly down onto the snowy ground.

'First,' said Nanuk, 'I shall show how to make a traditional snow igloo.'

Meg frowned. 'I thought *all* igloos were made of snow,' she said.

Nanuk shook his head. '*Iglu* is an Inuit word,' he explained. 'It simply means *house.*'

'There you are, Meg!' her dad laughed. 'You've

come all this way and you've been living in an igloo all your life.'

Meg turned back to Nanuk. 'But do you know how to make a . . . a *proper* igloo?' she asked.

'Yes, child,' he replied. 'I watched my grandfather, who watched *his* grandfather . . .' He sighed sadly, and began kicking at the newly fallen snow beneath his feet. 'Though, the weather is no longer what it was when my grandfather was alive,' he said. 'Fresh snow at this time of year . . . It's very strange.'

'The climate's changing all right,' said Meg's dad. 'It's warming up. I did a piece up in Alaska last year. The permafrost there is melting. Whole highways are buckling, houses are collapsing . . .'

'Then we must build our snow igloo as quickly as possible,' said Nanuk. 'Before it is too late.'

All four adults laughed, but Meg remained silent. What use would the old ways of surviving in snow and ice be, if that very snow and ice was all to melt?

'The snow beneath is packed hard by the

wind,' Nanuk was explaining. 'Firm to walk on and compact enough to keep its shape when cut into blocks.' He pulled a long steel knife from his belt and held it up. 'In the old days snow knives were made of caribou bone.'

Meg's dad nodded. 'That'll do nicely as an introduction,' he said. 'OK, places everyone. Ricky, Donna, we're going for a take.'

'Igloo Construction. Take one,' Donna announced, and slammed the clapper-board shut.

The camera scanned the snowy desolation before focusing in on Ted Sundberg. He smiled into the camera.

'While you're all snug and warm at home, I'm here on the northern reaches of Bolam Island where the temperatures can drop to as low as minus fifty degrees – that's twice as cold as your home freezer.' He laughed. 'Today, it's a relatively warm minus eight.'

He turned and looked round the Arctic landscape. The camera panned round with him, then returned to his face.

'Bleak and barren,' Ted Sundberg went on.

'Yet, in spite of the ferocity of the climate, the Inuit people have lived here for over a thousand years. They have managed not only to survive, but to prosper in a place where most of us would consider it impossible to live.'

Meg watched her dad proudly. Since she was a small girl she had watched him on television speaking from all over the world. The Kalahari Desert. The Amazon rain-forest. The top of Mount Everest. The bottom of the Atlantic. Ted Sundberg was a household name; to many, a hero.

'To survive such conditions there are four essentials: food, water, fire, and shelter,' he said. 'For all of these, one tool is absolutely vital. The snow knife.'

For a second time, Nanuk held his snow knife up.

'It can be used for skinning a caribou and chopping up the meat. For hacking out lumps of ice to be melted for drinking. For slicing the seal blubber used for fires. Last, but not least, it is used for cutting the blocks of snow from which the Inuit hunter builds his igloo.'

Meg looked round her. The majestic vastness stretched away in all directions and it occurred to her that it was this – the enormity of the place – which could never be captured on film. Whenever she saw her dad speaking from some far off corner of the Earth, she had the feeling that the place had somehow been tamed. If television cameras are there, it can't be *that* remote, she would say to herself. Now she knew she was wrong.

'The snow looks like blocks of polystyrene,' her dad was explaining to the camera. 'Once trimmed to the right shape, the latest piece is positioned, so – and pressed into place.'

The wind blew, and a dusting of the recent snow writhed like snakes across the frozen flatlands.

No, thought Meg, with a thrill of excitement. You have not been tamed.

Since he was working from inside the igloo, it soon became impossible for Nanuk to cut his own blocks. Meg's dad took over the task – and surprisingly well. Finally, he wedged the top piece into place.

'It's warm work,' Ted grinned into the camera. He tapped the side of the igloo and crouched down. 'As the builder is now inside, he must cut a door to get out.'

At that moment, the blade of the knife appeared in the side of the dome. A hole was cut, and Nanuk climbed out. The pair of them stood up.

'There you have it,' said Ted Sundberg. 'A snow igloo. Shelter from the wind and intense cold for those hunting on the ice.' He glanced at his watch, looked up and smiled. 'And complete in under forty-five minutes. How long did it take *you* to put up the family tent last time?'

He continued smiling.

'Cut!' said Donna.

Ted Sundberg switched off his smile. 'How was it?' he said.

'Fabulous!' said Donna.

'Excellent,' Ricky agreed. 'Though I want to get some long shots of the igloo when we set off, to give it all a sense of scale.'

'Good idea,' said Ted. 'I need to hammer home to the viewers the incredible resourcefulness of the Inuit people.' He turned back to Nanuk. 'Where to, now?' he said.

'For seal hunting?' said Nanuk. 'We must travel west.'

* * *

By the time they stopped for the final long-shot of the now tiny igloo, it was snowing. What started as a few flakes had rapidly turned into a dense and driving blanket of fine, granular snow. Meg climbed down from the snowmobile and wandered off a little way. The snow clung to the fur-lined jacket.

Meg was cold. Very cold. She began swinging her arms and stamping her feet to get the circulation going.

Then suddenly, she heard something. She stood stock-still. It was the same sound that she'd heard while watching the northern lights with Joe, but much louder: a heart-rending wail of utter desolation that echoed through the frozen air. Trembling anxiously she turned to Nanuk. The old man looked troubled.

'What is it?' she whispered.

Nanuk fixed her with his eyes. 'The old ways are dear to the spirits,' he said. 'Now that they are being forgotten, the spirits are growing restless.'

CHAPTER 5

Footprints

Seal hunting had to be put on hold that day. Not only did the thick snow make filming impossible, but it also covered up the seals' tell-tale breathing holes in the frozen ice.

'August,' said Nanuk glumly. 'I've never seen so much snow this early before. The wind direction's all wrong.' He paused. 'Follow me,' he said. 'There's something I want you to see.'

As the others went with him, Ted nodded to Ricky to start the camera rolling. He filmed Nanuk pointing down to a low tongue of wind-sculpted snow with his mittened hand.

'We call this an *ukuluraq*,' he explained. 'It points in the same direction as the wind.' He bent down and touched the edge of the ice-tongue. 'Knowing which way the winds usually blow at different times of the year, we are able to work out where north lies.'

'Compasses are useless so close to the magnetic north pole,' Ted Sundberg said into the camera. 'For this reason, hunters must have other methods – such as this ice-tongue – if they are not to get lost.'

He turned to Nanuk. 'Have *you* ever got lost?' he asked. The old man looked down modestly, and shook his head. Ted Sundberg nodded into the camera. 'So, it is possible to find your way, even in the bleakest of places – once you know how to read the signs.'

'Cut,' said Donna, and gave the thumbs-up sign.

'Of course,' he said to Meg as they walked back to the snowmobile. 'If the winds *do* change direction, the Inuit will have to re-learn everything. Just as well G.P.S. has been invented.'

Meg looked blank. 'G.P. . . .' she began.

'Global Positioning System,' he said, pulling a small black box from his inside pocket. He tapped into it, and a map appeared on the screen with co-ordinates: '73 point 39 degrees north by 80 point 08 degrees west,' he read off. 'Give or take a few metres.'

'But how does it work?' said Meg.

'Global beacons. Satellites,' her dad replied, stuffing the G.P.S. back inside the warmth of his jacket. 'We've got new technology to get us out of the scrape that the old technology has got us into.'

'So where does that leave Nanuk?' asked Meg.

'Lost, I guess,' he said and patted his pocket. 'Unless he buys one of these. Though heaven knows how many caribou and seal-skins it would cost!'

Meg turned and looked sadly at the old man. He was bent over, inspecting the ground intently.

'What have you found?' she asked.

Nanuk stood up and shook his head. 'I've never seen anything like it,' he said.

'What?' said Meg.

Nanuk nodded ahead. Meg looked. A series of marks in the snow disappeared off towards the mountains. Although the snowfall had all but filled them in, there was no doubt what they were. Animal footprints.

'They're not bear tracks,' said Nanuk. 'Or caribou . . .'

At that moment, the deep yet melancholy sound of wailing echoed far away in the distance. It was answered by another. And another. Meg shuddered uneasily. 'The spirits again?' she said.

Nanuk did not reply. He turned on his heels and trudged back to the snowmobile. Meg followed him. They both knew that spirits didn't leave footprints.

CHAPTER 6

Local colour

It took them over two hours to get back to
Prospect. The conditions were atrocious and, by
the time they arrived, the whole town was
shrouded in a fresh covering of white. Meg's dad
parked outside the Seal Cafe.

It was wonderfully warm inside the dimly-lit
cafe, and filled with the murmur of voices. A
stuffed seal lay in a glass case on one side of the
counter. Sepia photographs lined the walls.

'Joe!' said Meg, spotting her new friend seated
alone in the corner and eating a hamburger.
'Where were you this morning?'

'Oh, you know,' he said vaguely. 'Things to do . . .'

Meg heard Nanuk muttering angrily under his breath.

'Actually, Joe,' Meg's dad said, as he sat down beside him, 'you're just the person I was hoping to meet. Your grandad's going to take me through the Inuit method of treating caribou leather in one of the workshops this afternoon. I think it'll be a bit dull for Meg, so I was wondering if you could show her round Prospect.'

'I'd be glad to,' said Joe. 'Though it won't take long,' he added glumly.

Meg was pleased. It would give her a chance to talk to Joe about the strange howling cry she'd heard three times now. And after a big lunch of burgers, chips and milkshakes, the pair of them climbed to their feet.

'See you later, Dad,' said Meg.

'Have fun,' he replied. Then, just as she was following Joe to the door, he called out. 'And don't forget to keep your eyes peeled, Meg,' he said. 'Local colour, that's what I'm after. Anything that'll make your average TV viewer go *"Aaah!"* You get me?'

Meg winced. 'I get you,' she said, once again squirming with embarrassment. Her dad was behaving as if the people of Prospect were nothing more than quaint curiosities.

After the warmth of the cafe, it seemed colder than ever outside. Meg shivered and pulled up her hood. She turned to Joe.

'I'm sorry about my dad,' she said quietly. 'He doesn't mean to sound so patronizing.'

But Joe didn't seem bothered. 'I like your dad,' he said. 'There's no reason to be sorry. Anyway, look!'

Meg followed his gaze. Approaching from the opposite direction on a husky-drawn sled, was a young woman wearing a huge caribou-skin jacket. The hood was up, and out of it peered two faces. Hers and that of her baby, which was strapped to her back.

'Cute, or what?' said Joe. Meg laughed. 'And look over there!' he said. Meg turned to see an Arctic fox rummaging through the bins. As they got close, it scampered off. 'It's the polar bears you have to be careful of,' Joe said. 'When the weather's really bad they come into town looking for freebies. And they can be dangerous.'

The talk of bears reminded Meg of the tracks she and Nanuk had seen earlier – and the desolate wailing. Finally, she asked Joe about the mysterious cry she'd heard the night before. His reaction took her by surprise.

'So you heard it, too!' he exclaimed. 'I thought I'd imagined it. What do you think it was?'

'I hoped *you* were going to tell *me*,' said Meg.

Joe shrugged. 'I haven't a clue,' he said. 'It wasn't a bear. Or a caribou. Sometimes you can

hear the seals crying out in the bay, but . . . no, it wasn't them either.'

'Your grandad thinks it was spirits,' said Meg.

Joe looked down. 'I know what Grandad thinks,' he said sullenly. 'He thinks I'm turning my back on my ancestors. He thinks I've angered them.' He snorted. 'When I was little, Dad used to tell me stories about the sasquatch . . .'

'The *what*?' said Meg.

Joe laughed. 'Bigfoot. The yeti. The abominable snowman,' he said, raising his eyebrows in disbelief. 'Said it lived out there in the deepest wilderness where even the Inuit never ventured. A hairy creature – half-man, half-ape . . .'

Meg's eyes grew wide. 'Have you ever seen it?'

she asked.

'Course not,' said Joe. ''Cos it doesn't exist. And neither do Grandad's spirits.'

'But I saw footprints,' said Meg excitedly. 'Big and round and . . .'

'How many toes?' Joe interrupted.

'I . . . I'm not sure,' said Meg. 'It was snowing, and they were being filled in.'

'So they might not have been footprints at all,' said Joe.

Meg remembered the long line of tracks disappearing towards the distant mountains. 'They were footprints all right,' she said. '*Big* footprints . . .' She noticed Joe staring far into the distance, and paused. 'Joe? What is it?'

He turned towards her. 'There is one other possibility,' he said.

'There is?' said Meg. 'What?'

Joe sat forward. 'There's a research station north-west of here,' he explained. 'Near the mountains. Perhaps . . . I don't know, perhaps that howling cry is something to do with it.'

'A research station?' said Meg. 'But what's it doing here?'

Joe shrugged. 'No one knows. The whole place is sealed off. There's a high wire fence around three sides, with the wall of mountains at the back. Entry is strictly forbidden.'

Meg sighed. 'So you don't know anything about it?'

'Not really,' Joe admitted. 'It's owned by a big multinational company called Geo Exploration. They built the place – oh, eleven years ago, now. Sometimes you see helicopters heading in that direction. Sometimes a ship will dock in North Inlet. Otherwise, nothing.'

'Eleven years,' said Meg thoughtfully. 'I wonder what they've been doing all that time? And why up here, where it's so isolated?'

'Perhaps they needed to be somewhere cold. Or unpolluted. Or . . .

'Or maybe,' Meg interrupted, 'they've got something to hide.'

CHAPTER 7

Homing in

Everyone was up early the following day. The weather had improved enough for Nanuk to suggest that they set out on the seal hunting expedition again.

'And if we have no luck, then I'll take you further north and show you how to fish for birds!' he said.

'Birds!' said Meg.

'The Inuit use long-handled nets to trap birds,' her dad explained. 'Isn't that right, Nanuk?'

'It certainly is,' Nanuk said. 'But hopefully the

weather will stay good enough for seal hunting. We are running low on seal blubber,' he added.

'Whatever,' said Ted Sundberg. He turned to Meg. 'By the way, I called Mum earlier. She sends her love.'

'You called her from here!' said Meg, surprised.

'On my super-duper satellite phone,' he explained. 'It's fantastic! You can call from anywhere in the world . . .'

'If you're ready, Ted,' Donna called over. 'I think we should go for that take you wanted. The colours are amazing.'

Looking round, Meg saw what Donna meant. The combination of bright sun and dark clouds was spectacular. The snow and bare rocks gleamed like burnished silver and bronze, and the distant mountains were purple against the sky.

Ted Sundberg strolled over and took up position beside the snowmobile where Nanuk was sitting waiting.

'And, rolling,' said Donna. 'Seal Hunting. Departure. Take one.'

Ted smiled. 'The snowmobile comes in all shapes and sizes,' he said. 'This one is a three-seater. One thing is for sure, these vehicles have revolutionized the Inuits' lives. They are fast. They are powerful. And, and unlike huskies, a snowmobile neither barks nor chases the caribou away.'

He climbed up next to Nanuk.

'Today, though, we are not hunting caribou. Today, we are after seal.' He lowered his goggles, lifted the hood of his caribou-skin parka and the snowmobile drove off towards the horizon.

'Cut!' Donna yelled.

Five minutes later, everyone was ready for the real departure. Ted turned to his daughter. 'Would you mind going with Donna and Joe in the second snowmobile?' he said. 'There are one or two things I need to talk over with Nanuk before we film the seal hunt.'

'No, that's fine,' said Meg. She didn't add that Joe was exactly the person she wanted to travel with. It would give them a chance to make plans.

As they sped away into the vast expanse of glistening whiteness, Meg's heart thrilled. The skis whooshed. The air whistled past them. Apart from their own tracks, the snow was untouched. Meg imagined she was an explorer crossing the snowy wastes for the first time. Reckless, intrepid, and alone.

Far away to their right, Joe pointed out a family of polar bears; a mother and two cubs padding slowly across the ice. A little further on they stopped to watch an aerial battle between two birds fighting over a scrap of food. Their angry cries filled the air.

Joe and Meg looked at one another. 'No,' said

Joe. 'Whatever we heard, it wasn't birds.'

Meg shook her head. 'But it must have been something – or someone,' she said. She paused and when she spoke again it was more quietly – so that Donna wouldn't hear. 'How far is that research station?'

Joe glanced round. 'Why?' he said.

Meg shrugged. 'Nothing.'

'I told you,' said Joe. 'Entry is strictly forbidden.'

'Oh, I wasn't planning on going *in*,' Meg whispered. 'I just thought we might find some more footprints. Clearer ones. Or . . . I don't know. Some kind of clue.'

'I see,' said Joe.

They sped on across the icy wasteland in silence. It was almost two hours later when Joe pointed towards a tiny black dot in the distance. As it came nearer, Meg saw that it was a wooden hut standing on the edge of a frozen lake.

'Much easier than making a snow-igloo every hunting expedition,' said Joe with a grin.

The snowmobiles were parked up and, with the film running and microphones on, Nanuk and Ted Sundberg set out onto the ice.

'The seals swim beneath the surface of the ice,' Ted was explaining to the camera, 'but, being mammals, they have to come up for air. You can spot their breathing holes because of the mounds of snow. If you find one, a quick sniff reveals how recently it has been used.'

Nanuk paused and knelt down in the snow. He breathed in and nodded. 'This one smells of fish,' he said. 'A seal was here not long ago.' He poked around in the hole with his spear.

'Seals make tunnels in the ice at an angle,' Ted Sundberg continued. 'And the hunter must work out which direction the seal is likely to come from. You only get one chance at a kill.'

Keeping out of camera-shot, Meg watched Nanuk take up his position beside the air-hole. He stood, knees bent and arm raised, with his spear at the ready. And there he stayed.

The minutes passed. Half an hour . . . Nanuk remained motionless by the hole. Meg turned away and walked over to Joe. 'So how long *does* this take?' she asked.

Joe shrugged. 'Four or five hours on average. Then, if you're lucky, he might catch a seal. You'll be able to watch the ritual method of cutting the animal's head off – to release its spirit,' he explained.

Meg pulled a face.

'Or we *could* go for a spin in the snowmobile,' Joe suggested.

Meg looked round. 'Where were you thinking of going?'

'The research station isn't far from here,' he said, with a grin. 'We could look for those clues. If you still want to . . .'

Meg's heart pounded with excitement. Of course she still wanted to!

* * *

With one less person on board, the snowmobile went even faster than before, hissing over the surface. And when a fine snow began to fall it was as though they had taken off and were swooping through the sky.

'Keep your eyes peeled,' Joe said. 'I need to concentrate.'

Further and further into the polar landscape they went. The mountains grew nearer yet, as the snow thickened, less visible. Meg stared all round her. Now she felt truly cut off. The hut had long since disappeared and the snow was closing in. She shivered uneasily.

Suddenly, out of the corner of her eye, Meg sensed movement. She spun round and squinted into the snowy distance. And there it was. Something tall and shaggy was shambling away from them.

'Look!' she screamed. 'Over there!'

Joe steered sharply to the left. 'I see it!' he said. He gasped. 'But what on earth is it?'

CHAPTER 8

Lost in the snow

The chase was on. With his foot down, Joe sped
after the huge, shambling creature. Yet even as
they watched, it disappeared. The snow was just
too thick.

'It's got away,' said Meg disappointedly.

Joe slowed down. 'We'll follow its tracks,' he
said.

Meg stared round her anxiously. 'Shouldn't
we be getting back?' she said.

'When we're so close?' said Joe. 'Is that really
what you want?'

'Of course not!' Meg snapped. 'But, look at it.'

The snow was thicker than the day before. Even Joe had to admit that it was bad.

'Tell you what,' he said. 'We'll go on for ten minutes. Then, if we can't find it, we'll head back.'

Meg nodded uneasily. 'OK, then,' she said.

Joe advanced slowly along the line of footprints. 'That's odd,' he said. 'I could have sworn that what we saw was up on two legs.'

'Me, too,' said Meg.

'Well, these tracks definitely belong to a *four*-legged animal,' he said. 'And a big one, by the look of it.'

At first the tracks were easy to follow. Yet it wasn't long before they had become so blurred that Meg and Joe were arguing over which way to go. And all the time the heavy snow closed in around the snowmobile.

'I really think we ought to be getting back now,' said Meg.

This time Joe did not argue. He swung the snowmobile round until they were facing the way they'd come.

Then he braked.

Meg looked at him, her heart thumping. 'We're lost, aren't we?'

'Of course not,' said Joe hotly. 'I know exactly where I am. It's just . . . I'm not quite sure where the hut is.'

Meg was furious. She was also frightened. The snow was already beginning to drift up against the snowmobile, and Joe's refusal to learn about the old ways suddenly seemed short-sighted, foolish.

'So what do we do?' she said.

'I think we should head for the mountains,' said Joe. 'We're quite near them, and we can shelter there until the snow eases off.'

Meg nodded. Angry though she was, she had no choice but to trust Joe. He started up the snowmobile and sped off in the direction of the now invisible mountains. Meg's teeth chattered, not only with the growing cold, but also with fear. And as they ploughed on into the never-ending blanket of white, that fear grew.

What if they were heading in the wrong direction? If only she could see something. If only the snow would stop falling so that she could convince herself that there was still something there *to* see!

'Not far now,' said Joe, encouragingly.

But Meg did not believe him. He was trying to humour her. He was trying to hide the awful truth that they were lost forever. And when the dark wall of rock loomed up in front of her, she still found it hard to believe that they had reached the mountains – until Joe cried out.

'We've made it,' he shouted triumphantly.

He slowed down, veered to the right and drove along the rocks in an easterly direction, taking care not to hit one of the many boulders half hidden beneath the snow drifts. Above them, a tall finger of rock – higher than the rest – pointed up towards the sky. Below it was a jutting crag shaped like a lion's head. And below that . . .

'There!' said Meg, waving a mittened hand towards a gaping black hole in the rock. 'A cave.'

Joe nodded and pulled up on the sheltered side of a massive slab of fallen rock. The two of them jumped out.

'Come on,' said Joe. 'Let's get to that cave

before . . .'

'MMWNAAAAAAAA!!!'

The pair of them froze in mid-stride. The cry came again. Louder this time, and ending with a trailing wail of desolation. Meg clutched hold of Joe and stared round her.

'MMMWNAAAAAAAAA-OOOO!!!'

The terrifying noise ripped through the air for a third time. It bounced off the rock-face and echoed eerily in the dark recesses.

'MMMWNA-A-A-A-A-A-A-A-A!!!'

CHAPTER 9

Trapped

'Do you think it's actually *in* the cave?' Meg whispered.

Joe shook his head as, once again, the desperate cry resounded. 'It's over there somewhere,' he said. 'And I think it's heading away from us.'

'Well, the snow's too thick for us to track it,' said Meg. 'And we can't stay here.'

Joe agreed and, as the agonized cry of the strange beast grew fainter, the pair of them scrambled hurriedly up the rocky slope to the cave entrance. Meg pulled out her torch and shone it inside.

'It looks fine,' she said.

Joe sniffed the air. 'And there haven't been any animals here,' he said. 'At least, not recently.'

Dry and protected from the wind, the cave felt warm after the bitter chill outside. Joe removed the knapsack from his back and unpacked it.

'Primus-stove, matches, saucepan, mugs, plates, spoons . . .' he rattled off. 'And . . . let me see.' He inspected the packets of dried soup. 'Country vegetable and minestrone,' he said. 'We can mix them together.' He climbed to his feet. 'I'll go and see about some water.'

While he was gone, Meg looked around the cave. It was bigger than she'd first thought, stretching far back into the mountainside. Then she heard Joe calling her.

'Coming,' she replied, her voice echoing loudly all round her.

At the entrance of the cave, Joe had lit the primus and was melting a large chunk of ice in the saucepan. Ten minutes later they were

tucking into bowls of hot soup and oat-cakes.
And when that was gone, Meg
melted more ice for some
drinking chocolate.

Now that she was warm and her stomach was
full, she was feeling much more confident. Joe
stood looking out of the cave.

'Any sign of you-know-what?' she asked.

'No,' said Joe. We must have scared it off.' He
turned round and frowned. 'Odd,' he said. 'The
steam from the saucepan is being drawn back
into the cave . . .'

Just then, the pair of them heard something
deep inside the tunnel. Joe spun round and

shone the light into the shadows. Two gleaming yellow eyes stared back.

Meg squeaked with surprise. It was a dog, huge and fierce, which snarled at them through bared teeth.

'Easy, lad,' came a voice, and a tall, heavily-built man in a black uniform appeared. On his jacket was a badge bearing his name: *Mulligan*. He strode towards them. 'This is Geo Exploration property,' he said. 'A restricted area.'

'We . . . I . . . that is . . .' Joe stammered.

'We were on a trip to the frozen lake to watch his grandad seal hunting,' Meg explained. 'But we got lost in the blizzard.'

'And what are you doing on Bolam Island in the first place?' the man asked her suspiciously. 'You're no Eskimo.'

'I'm here with my father,' Meg replied. 'We're . . .' She hesitated. Security at the research station was clearly extremely tight. She thought it unwise to mention that her dad was making a documentary. 'We're on holiday,' she said.

'Yeah?' the guard sneered. 'Well, you can't stay here.'

'We can't leave before the blizzard stops,' said Meg.

The guard looked outside the cave. The snow was thicker than ever. He turned back to Meg and Joe.

'You'd better come with me,' he said gruffly.

As they followed the guard, Meg realized how strongly the narrow tunnel smelled of soup. Probably that was what had alerted the guard – or rather his dog – in the first place.

After fifty metres or so, they came to a steel door. Meg looked round. At this point, the cave was no longer natural. Tell-tale jagged swirls in the side of the tunnel showed that a rotating cutter had been used to drill into the rock. Mulligan used a swipe-card, and the door opened with a click. He ordered Joe and Meg inside and led them along the warm corridor.

Although the tunnel was round, the corridor they found themselves in was square – an internal shell, flatly lit with hidden lighting. Despite the ventilation grilles every ten metres, the air smelled antiseptic. The whole place hummed as if from a distant generator.

Meg looked at the doors as the guard hurried them along the corridor. Most had meaningless numbers or letters on them – *O2/b.c.; 07/p.u.* A few, however, were all too chillingly clear. *Rat Laboratory (I & II)*. And *Monkey Laboratory*.

Meg shuddered. Whatever Geo Exploration was up to, it involved experiments on animals.

'Don't dawdle,' the guard called back and Meg trotted to catch up. A little further on they came to a wide octagonal area where several of the corridors met. Men with clipboards and women in white coats were hurrying this way and that. The guard led them to a door opposite. *Recreation Room*, Meg read.

'Wait here until I find someone to deal with you,' he said.

As he closed the door, Meg and Joe heard the sound of a key turning in the lock. Meg snorted. 'As if we had a choice!'

CHAPTER 10

Professor von Klett

Some five minutes later, they heard the door-handle being rattled, followed by the sound of a key in the lock. Meg and Joe looked up expectantly. The door opened and a short, balding man came in.

'Never find a thing when you need it,' he was muttering. 'Turn your back for a moment, and everything's been cleared away.' He reached the bookcase and bent down to look at the lowest shelf. 'No, no, no,' he said, as he flicked his way along the row of plastic binders. 'Aha! I *knew* it! Confounded meddlers . . .'

He pulled out a binder and looked through the magazines it contained. Meg cleared her throat. The man spun round.

'Oh, my goodness!' he exclaimed as he realized for the first time that he was not alone. 'You made me jump.'

'Sorry,' said Meg. 'But we were locked up in here and told to wait.'

'Locked up?' the man said. 'By whom?'

'Mulligan,' said Meg, remembering the name-badge. 'The guard who found us in the cave,' she said, and went on to tell him everything that had happened.

'But this is dreadful,' the man said when she had finished. 'Our first visitors in eleven years and you're treated like common criminals. It's time to put matters right. My name is Professor Wilhelm von Klett,' he said, and held out his hand. 'I am in charge of research and development.'

'I'm Meg Sundberg,' said Meg, as the professor pumped her arm up and down.

'And I'm Joe. Joe Palituk.'

'Pleased to meet you both,' said the professor. 'Now, come. Let me get you some refreshments.'

As the professor led them from the room, Meg and Joe caught one another's eye. Meg raised her eyebrows questioningly. Joe shrugged. They could only hope that the professor was as friendly as he seemed.

'There we are,' said the professor, back in his office, as he poured them all steaming mugs of hot tea. 'Help yourselves to biscuits. Then you must tell me all about yourselves. It's been so long since I talked to anyone new!'

As they chatted on, both Joe and Meg took care not to give too much away. Joe told him about his life in Prospect. Meg told him about her trip to Bolam Island, explaining that she and her father were interested in the local wildlife.

The professor smiled. 'I myself deal with animals,' he said.

'Yes,' said Meg, turning away. 'I saw the names on the doors. Rats. Monkeys . . .'

'We need them for our experiments,' the professor said.

Joe looked confused. 'I don't understand,' he said.

'He means,' said Meg, prickling, 'that animals are killed here in the name of science.'

If the professor was put out by the bluntness of her words, he did not show it. 'It's true,' he said. 'We have performed controlled experiments on some laboratory animals. Mice, mainly. Yet make no mistake, Meg, my aim is to create life not to destroy it.' He paused. 'But then why am I telling you all this?' he said, and smiled. 'I suppose it's what comes of being cut off for so long.'

Meg smiled back uncertainly. 'What do you mean, *to create life*?' she asked, scarcely daring to believe that the professor would answer.

But answer, he did. Now that the professor had started, it seemed there was no stopping him.

'I believe passionately that something must be done to stop animals becoming extinct. Of course, there have always been periods when living organisms have faced mass extinction. Take 65 million years ago, for instance. Thirty-three per cent of all plant and animal species vanished off the face of the Earth.'

'When the Earth was struck by a meteor,' said Meg.

'That's one theory,' said the professor. He sighed. 'Now it is happening again. We are on the brink of a disaster. But this time the situation has been caused by humans. We are altering the environment. We are changing the weather. We are losing species after species. As the problem is human-made, it is up to humans to find a solution. And I, Professor Wilhelm von Klett have perfected that solution. Now anything is possible,' he said. 'Anything at all.'

He paused. Meg and Joe waited for an explanation.

'The answer,' he said softly, 'is cloning.'

'What's cloning?' asked Joe.

'It is the creation of a perfect copy of any species by using one single cell from the original animal or plant,' the professor explained. 'Come, I'll show you.' He laughed. 'I don't often get the chance to . . . to show off. Prepare to be amazed!'

CHAPTER 11

Geo Exploration

Despite the professor's words, nothing could have prepared Meg for what she and Joe saw as they were taken on their guided tour of the research station. First of all, they found themselves in a long laboratory lined with stainless steel cabinets and glass-fronted pods.

'This is where we prepare the cells,' the professor explained. 'It's a tricky business,' he said, and went on to describe the process in language so technical that Meg's head was soon reeling.

'It's no good, Professor,' she said finally. 'I just

don't understand.'

Professor von Klett looked down at her. 'I'm sorry,' he said. 'I'll try to make it simpler . . . First of all, we take a cell from the donor animal. Then the nucleus – that's the part right at the centre – is removed. Each nucleus contains an entire set of chromosomes – the genetic code for the new animal. With me so far?'

Meg nodded. 'I think so,' she said. The professor went on.

'Then, this nucleus is injected into a fertilized egg whose own nucleus has been taken out. An electric current is passed through the egg to stimulate fusion and growth.'

'Fusion?' said Meg.

'The host egg must accept the new nucleus as its own,' the professor explained. 'At the moment, we are only successful in less than one per cent of cases. But we are getting better all the time.' He smiled at Meg. 'Soon, we shall be able to go into into full-scale production.'

Meg shivered. 'It makes it sound like a factory,' she said.

The professor's expression grew serious.

'Without my work, we could soon see a world without rhinos or pandas, tigers or tortoises, gorillas or chimpanzees . . . They are all on the edge of extinction. But I can save them, Meg. I can make sure that your grandchildren – and your grandchildren's grandchildren – will experience the world that you and I love so much. And if that involves a little *manufacturing*, am I wrong to do it?'

Meg looked down. She felt embarrassed. 'N . . . no,' she faltered.

'Have you cloned gorillas, then?' said Joe. 'I've always wanted to see a gorilla . . .'

'One step at a time, Joe,' the professor laughed. 'First I'll show you the results of my earliest experiments.'

As the three of them returned to the corridor and headed back the way they'd come, Meg couldn't stop thinking about the curious creature they'd seen and heard on the snow. Could *that* have something to do with the professor's work?

They came to one of the doors Meg had noticed earlier. It was marked, *O2/b.c.* She followed the professor and Joe inside. The whole room echoed with the sound of croaking. Meg stepped forward and peered into one of the glass pods.

'Frogs!' she said.

'Natterjack toads, to be precise,' said the professor. '*Bufo calamita*. These toads – which are facing extinction in the wild – were my breakthrough. From two individuals, I have created more than a thousand of each. We have already released some back into the wild. More will follow. The natterjack has been saved.'

'Amazing,' Meg breathed. 'So the letters on the door: *b.c.* – they must stand for *Bufo calamita*. What does *p.u.* stand for?'

The professor smiled. 'Follow me, and I'll show you,' he said.

Meg's heart raced. Were they about to see the creature that she and Joe had seen and heard?

'The snow leopard, *Panthera uncia*,' the professor announced as they entered the room marked *07/p.u.* 'Like the natterjack, once faced with extinction.'

Along the length of the room, the walls were

lined with cages. There was a snow leopard inside each one. They snarled at the three human visitors, and Meg shuddered. She hated seeing wild animals caged up, and was about to ask when they would be set free when the professor's pager bleeped.

'I won't be a minute,' he said. 'Feel free to look around.' And with that, he scurried to the telephone by the door.

Meg stood staring at the snow leopard in front of her. It was magnificent, with a pale grey coat, decorated with black rosettes and smaller spots, and a black streak running along its spine. It stared back at Meg, and yowled.

'Poor thing,' she said. 'It won't always be like this. They're going to send you to the mountains. You'll love it there.'

The snow leopard yowled again and turned its back on her. Meg knew there and then, that this was not the creature they had seen and heard outside in the snow.

She became suddenly aware of the professor's raised voice.

'Of course they're the same, Simkiss,' he was shouting. 'They're clones!'

Meg sidled closer, and listened. She could hear the muffled sound of the voice at the other end. It seemed angry. She moved closer still.

'Yes, yes,' the professor said quietly. 'I do realize that Geo Exploration is just one branch of Geo International. Yes, and I also understand that Mr Baker is running a business not a charity.' He sighed wearily. 'I will do the best I can.'

The voice at the other end spoke again. The professor gasped.

'He's coming *here*?' he said. 'Now? And he said *what*? But that is my life's work. My *meisterwerk*. He couldn't . . . You wouldn't . . .'

The line went dead.

The professor stood for a moment, with the receiver in his hand. He looked pale and shaken.

'Are you all right?' Meg asked.

'Yes, I'm . . .' He put the telephone down. 'The patterns on their coats,' he muttered. 'They're all the same. And now he's threatening . . .' He removed his glasses, wiped them briskly with his handkerchief, put them back on and looked up. 'Meg, Joe,' he said, as he opened the door for them. 'It has been a pleasure, but I'm afraid our little tour must come to an end.'

Meg groaned softly. The information about his work had been fascinating – but she was still none the wiser about the weird creature outside.

'Professor,' she said boldly. 'There's just one more thing . . .'

'*There* you are!' came an angry voice. Meg and Joe spun round to see Mulligan. 'Where have you been?' he demanded. 'I locked the door.'

'And I *un*locked it,' the professor broke in. 'Meg Sundberg and Joe Palituk are my guests. I have been showing them my work . . .'

'You've *what*?' the guard said. 'Professor, do I have to remind you that everything which takes place in this research station is classified information? It is my job to prevent any breaches in security, and you . . .'

'They're just a couple of kids,' said the professor.

'I will have to report your actions to Mr Simkiss,' the guard said. He turned to Meg and Joe. 'Now, you two. Follow me.'

'Goodbye, Professor,' they both said, as the guard took them back down the humming corridors.

The professor waved half-heartedly, and turned away. He looked a very worried man.

'Keep up!' the guard snapped.

Meg hurried after him; *m.m./06/12; r.d./09; c.p./08* – the names on the doors flashed past.

Now she would never find out what secrets lay hidden behind them.

At the end of the corridor, the guard stopped. He opened the door and nodded outside.

'The snow's stopped,' he said simply.

Meg and Joe stepped out. The steel door

slammed shut behind them.

'Phew,' said Joe. 'For a moment I thought they were going to keep us locked up or something.'

Meg nodded. She too was glad that they were free to go. And yet, as she stepped outside, her relief vanished in an instant. There was no tunnel. No cave. In front of them lay an endless expanse of wind-blown whiteness. They had come out of a different door from the one they had gone in through.

'Joe!' she gasped. 'Where are we?'

CHAPTER 12

Snowbound

With her heart hammering in her chest, Meg turned and pounded her mittened fists against the steel door.

'Open it up!' she screamed. 'You can't leave us out here! You just can't.' She felt Joe's hand on her shoulder.

'It's no good,' he said. 'No one can hear you.'

Meg let her hands drop down by her side. Inside the research station, the combination of central heating and Inuit clothes had left her feeling hot and uncomfortable. Now, as the icy wind howled, it chilled her to the bone – and her growing terror made her shake all the more.

'Th . . . they've dumped us,' she stammered.

Joe looked round, his brow furrowed. He scanned the horizon and stared closely at the range of mountains with its peaks and cliffs. Finally he spoke.

'That way's west,' he said, nodding towards the sun. 'Which means that Prospect is in *that* direction,' he said, and pointed off across the snowy plains.

'Thank heavens for that,' said Meg. 'I was beginning to think we'd gone right through the rock to the other side of the mountains.'

Joe turned to her. He looked pale, worried. 'The question is, Meg, how do we get there?'

Meg gasped. How could she have been so stupid? The snowmobile was nowhere to be seen, and without it . . . 'Oh, Joe,' she said. 'What on earth do we do now?'

'That's what I was wondering,' he said. He looked round again. 'We left the snowmobile near the cave, didn't we? And there was a pointed rock above the cave. Do you remember?'

'Yes,' said Meg excitedly. 'It looked like a finger pointing upwards. And beneath it was another rock – like a lion's head.'

'Right,' said Joe. 'All we've got to do is look out for them. They can't be too far away.'

Meg looked along the range of mountains. On one side, was a jutting outcrop of rock; on the other, the cliff curved away into the distance. 'So which way do we go?' she asked. 'Left or right?'

'Neither,' said Joe. 'We walk back onto the plain. It'll give us a better view of the whole range.'

Meg nodded. Although she didn't like the idea of leaving the shelter of the rocks, she knew it was their only hope. Without another word, she set off. Joe tramped after her. As they rounded the furthest point of the jutting rock, Meg suddenly cried out.

'Look!'

Joe spun round, and the pair of them stared back at the cluster of buildings at the base of the mountains to their left. The whole area was surrounded by a high fence.

'That's it!' he said. 'The research station.'

'It's bigger than I thought it would be,' said Meg. She frowned. 'So where exactly were *we*?'

'I'm not sure,' said Joe. 'In the system of tunnels behind the buildings at a guess.'

'But that still doesn't tell us where the cave we went in through is,' said Meg.

Joe shook his head and turned back to the snowy desolation. 'Come on,' he said. 'Let's keep going until we see that pointed rock.'

As they trudged on across the snow and ice, Meg tightened her hood and thrust her hands

deep inside the caribou-skin parka. Although it had stopped snowing, the wind was as relentless as before. It howled and whined and chilled her to the bones.

'That Professor von Klett!' said Joe, with a whistle of admiration. 'He's a genius. Grandad's always going on about how the numbers of animals are dropping. Seals. Whales. Walruses. Caribou . . . Well, now he won't have to worry any more, will he? Not enough caribou? No problem, we'll just make a few more. Brilliant!'

Meg sighed. 'But isn't it sad that the

professor's work is necessary at all,' she said. 'I mean, a world without pandas . . .'

'Or gorillas,' added Joe.

'And when they've all died out, that's it,' she said. 'They're gone. Forever.'

'That's why the professor's work is so important,' said Joe.

Meg nodded. 'You're right,' she said. 'We'll just have to hope he's successful.' She paused and glanced back at the mountains. The wind slapped her face. There was still no sign of the pointed rock. 'So what *do* you think the creature we saw was?' she said.

'I've no idea,' said Joe. 'What's more, it doesn't look as though we'll ever find out.'

They continued in silence. Meg walked with her head down. It was easier to keep going if she couldn't see the endless, snowy plain stretching out in front of her. Apart from the wind, the only sound was the crunch and creak of the snow below their feet as they tramped slowly onwards. Then, all at once, Joe grabbed her arm.

'There it is!' he said. Meg looked round to see the tall pinnacle silhouetted against the sky.

'That *is* the one, isn't it?' said Joe.

'No doubt about it,' said Meg. 'Come on.'

The ferocious wind was hitting them head-on now. It snatched at their breath, it lashed at their faces and stung their eyes. Around her mouth, the fur of Meg's hood glistened with crystals of frost. Her legs felt like two lead weights. Only the thought of climbing back into the snowmobile kept her going.

She raised her head and stared again at the rock. Beneath it, the lion's head was becoming visible. Although it was hard to believe, they must be getting closer. She turned to Joe.

'Soon be there,' she shouted into the whistling wind.

But Joe did not reply. Staring ahead at the mountain peaks, he looked worried.

'What is it?' she said. And then she saw. The pinnacle had disappeared into a dense blanket of white that had crept over the mountain tops.

'It's more snow,' said Joe. 'Quick!'

The pair of them broke into a run, heading for the place where they had last seen the finger of rock. Ahead of them, the snowfall swept down the rockface and across the plain towards them. All at once, it struck.

Meg gasped. The air hissed. Her face felt as if it was being stabbed by a million needles. She could see nothing. Nothing at all. Reaching out desperately, she found Joe's hand and held it tightly. And together, the pair of them struggled on blindly in what they could only hope was the right direction.

If she had been on her own, Meg would not have made it. Her feet had gone numb and she couldn't stop shaking. She wanted to rest. Luckily, Joe knew the dangers of pausing, even for a moment. Every time Meg slowed down, he gripped her hand all the tighter and pulled her forwards.

'Nearly there,' he said encouragingly.

'You said that last time,' Meg muttered. '*And* the time before that.'

Joe nodded, but said nothing. He knew how easy it was to get lost when the snow robbed you of your sight. That was why, rather than risk wandering round in circles, the Inuit would build a snow igloo where they were. For the first time in his life, Joe Palituk was sorry that he didn't know more about the old ways.

Suddenly, he felt Meg clutching at his arm. 'What's that?' she said.

'What?' said Joe. 'I can't see anything.'

'Not see,' said Meg. 'Hear.' She cocked her head to one side.

It was difficult to make out anything above the sound of the howling wind and hissing snow. Yet as they stood there, ears pricked, they both heard it: a high-pitched trilling sound.

'It's Dad's satellite mobile!' Meg called back as she dashed towards the sound. 'Quick! Before they ring off.'

They stumbled upon the snowmobile almost at once. It was barely ten metres off. Because of the blinding snow, however, they might as well have been a thousand miles away and if it hadn't been for the ringing telephone, they would have passed it without knowing.

Meg found the mobile in her dad's padded jacket, which was tucked away under the seat. She pulled out the ringing phone, unfolded the receiving dish and pressed to receive the call.

'Hello?' she shouted into the mouthpiece. 'HELLO!'

'Meg!' came her dad's voice. 'Thank God you're all right. Where are you?'

'Oh, Dad!' said Meg. She was close to tears. 'It was awful. We got lost in the snow. We . . .'

'It's all right, Meg,' he said calmly. 'You're not lost now. If you look in the other side pocket, you'll find my G.P.S.. Do you remember? The Global Positioning System I showed you yesterday.'

'Yes, yes,' Meg said. She removed the little black box from the side pocket. 'I've got it,' she said. 'But the screen's blank.'

'Press the top left-hand button twice,' her dad instructed.

Meg did as she was told. With the first press, the screen began glowing. With the second, a map reference appeared.

'Yes!' she cried. 'It's 74 point 02 degrees north. And 80 point 1 . . .'

'MMMWNAAAAAAAAA-OOOO!!!'

The sudden noise took Meg completely by surprise. She jumped back. The satellite phone slipped out of her hand and fell with a crash onto the rocky ground. The red light went out.

'W . . . w . . . what is it?' she heard Joe whisper.

Meg looked away from the broken phone and stared in disbelief at the massive, shambling creature with its long ragged hair standing before her.

'It's the professor's *meisterwerk*,' she breathed. 'You were right, Joe. He *is* a genius.'

CHAPTER 13

A cry from the past

From her position behind the rock, Meg stared at the creature, open-mouthed. Her heart pounded. Her head spun. All at once, two more of them loomed out of the storm, lumbered across the snow and ice, and stood beside the first.

'What are elephants doing here?' said Joe.

'They're not elephants,' said Meg quietly.

'But . . .' Joe began.

'They're mammoths,' she told him.

'Mammoths?' he repeated.

'Mammoths,' said Meg, and a shiver tingled

up and down her spine. She knew that the last one had died out over 10,000 years earlier. Yet here were three magnificent specimens, extinct no longer. Somehow, the professor must have managed to bring them back from the dead.

Although not yet fully grown, the mammoths were well over two metres tall, and more powerfully built than any elephant. There were other differences, too. Each had a prominent hump on its back. Their ears were smaller, their trunks longer, and their eyes were far higher in their heads. Two of them had tusks which were already long and curving outwards.

'Why are they so hairy?' said Joe.

'To keep warm,' said Meg. 'They live . . . lived in cold climates.'

Joe nodded thoughtfully. 'And there was me, thinking that the sasquatch might exist after all,' he said.

' 'Fraid not,' said Meg, shaking her head. 'No sasquatch, no yeti, no abominable snowman – though you can see why we were fooled. All that long, shaggy hair,' she said. 'And from the back they really do look as if they're walking on two legs.' She paused. 'They're incredible!'

The snow had eased off and the three mammoths were tramping about on the spot, trumpeting uneasily.

'But I don't understand,' said Joe. 'If they died out so long ago, how come they're here now?'

'I don't know,' Meg admitted. In her mind, she went over the cloning procedure that the professor had outlined. Somehow, somewhere, he must have found some living mammoth cells.

All at once, Meg was startled to hear a distant throbbing sound. *Chugga-chugga-chugga*. The mammoths heard it, too. Their eyes rolled. They became restless. And, as one, they raised their trunks and bellowed.

'A helicopter!' Joe shouted and dived to the ground.

Meg ducked down beside him. 'I wonder if that's the head of the Geo company arriving?' she said, remembering the professor's telephone conversation.

As the helicopter disappeared behind the range of mountains, the noise faded. But the mammoths remained agitated.

'Let's get out of here,' said Joe nervously. He jumped into the snowmobile. 'Get in, Meg,' he cried.

But Meg could not move. She could only stare in horror as the mammoths started towards them, heads down, trunks extended, gathering speed. Joe fumbled with the switches on the dashboard, and all at once the full-beam of the headlight blazed ahead.

The mammoths roared with fury. Two of them reared up on their hind legs. The third trampled the snowy ground where it stood. And then they were off again, charging headlong at the snowmobile.

'RUN!' Meg screamed.

Joe didn't need to be told twice. He leaped from his seat, and ran for his life. Suddenly it wasn't as though the mammoths had been brought to life in the present; it was as though they – Meg and Joe – had been hurled back into the past. There they were in the middle of this snowy wasteland, face to face with creatures only cavemen had ever seen.

Meg and Joe made it to the cover of a line of rocks and boulders just as the mammoths reached the snowmobile. There they watched helplessly as the massive beasts vented their fury on the curious shining creature before them. They trampled it, kicked it and gored it with their tusks. Then, with a tumultuous roar, the largest of the three wrapped its massive trunk around the wreckage, lifted the whole lot up into the air and dashed it to the ground.

'MMMWNAAAAAAAAA!!!' The mammoths trumpeted victoriously.

Meg trembled with fear. Not only did she now know how dangerous the mammoths could be, but the frenzied creatures had destroyed their only means of escape. She could only hope that her dad had heard enough of the map reference to find them. Peering through a gap in the rocks she saw the mammoths, calm once more, trundling off, back the way they'd come.

'They're going,' Meg whispered. 'Shall we wait in the cave?'

'Might as well,' said Joe, climbing to his feet. The next instant he dropped back down. 'Then again, maybe not!'

Meg looked up. There were three men standing in the cave entrance. One of them had a pair of binoculars. 'There they are!' he shouted.

Joe was about to give himself up, but Meg held him back.

'They don't mean us,' she said. 'They're after the mammoths.'

He looked back up at the cave. It was true. All three guards were looking out across the plain. One of them pulled a radio from his pocket and spoke into it. Seconds later, Meg and Joe heard the rumble of approaching engines.

Peeking out from their hiding place, they saw three huge motorized sledges sweeping across the snow. Meanwhile, the guards in the cave had scrambled down the rock face and were running after the mammoths. Each one was carrying a rifle.

Oddly, the mammoths did not run off. Instead, they turned on their attackers and charged. Seeing what was happening, the men on the giant sledges flashed their lights and sounded their horns in an attempt to distract the furious creatures. But in vain. The mammoths had their sights on the three men, now down on one knee, rifles raised to their eyes.

'Now!' came a voice, and all three weapons went off.

The mammoths didn't even pause. They continued charging at the guards. Thirty metres. Twenty. Ten . . . Suddenly, one of the giant sledges drove between them. The three men jumped on the back, and the sledge-driver sped off.

Incensed, the mammoths raised their trunks and roared. Their trumpeting voices echoed round the mountains. Then one – the smallest – began to stagger. It lowered its head, tottered to one side, and collapsed. It wasn't long before the other two did the same.

Meg realized that the rifles had been loaded with tranquillizer darts, not bullets. The guards hadn't missed after all, and now all three of the magnificent mammoths were out for the count.

'We've got twenty minutes to get them back inside their enclosure,' one of the men shouted.

'Twenty minutes!'

The whole place erupted into a frenzy of activity. The three sledge machines were parked next to the sleeping mammoths. Harnesses were attached. Ramps lowered. Winches operated. And when the creatures had been secured into position, the guards jumped up onto the back of the sledges, and they were off.

A lump formed in Meg's throat. She turned to Joe. 'Come on,' she said. 'Let's get to the cave.'

'In a second,' said Joe. 'There's something I want to check out.' And before Meg could say anything, he had sprinted off towards the patch of trampled snow.

Three minutes later, he was back.

'Look!' he announced, showing Meg what he had found. 'It's a tranquillizer dart. I saw one of the guards dropping it. And with this . . .' He showed her the length of tubing from the smashed snowmobile. 'We've got a blow-pipe. Just in case.'

'In case of what?' said Meg.

'In case there are any more surprises waiting for us,' said Joe, grimly.

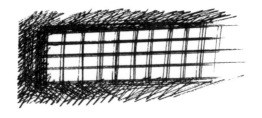

CHAPTER 14

Inside the mountain

Back in the cave, Meg was shivering. 'I hope the others get here quickly,' she muttered.

'It's going to take them some time,' said Joe. 'Unless your dad's got another one of those phones, he must have been calling from the General Store in Prospect.'

'No, he's only got the one,' said Meg.

'In that case, it's going to take them three hours or so,' he said.

'Three hours!' Meg gasped.

'Longer, if the weather gets any worse,' said Joe.

'But I can't wait that long,' Meg protested. 'I'm so cold.'

Joe shrugged. 'There is *one* place that's warmer,' he said, nodding back into the cave.

'Inside the institute?' said Meg. 'But how? The doors are made of heavy steel.'

Joe grinned. 'Who said anything about the doors?' He pulled out his pocket-light and switched it on. 'Follow me,' he said.

As they made their way down the tunnel, Joe explained what he had planned. Since the drilled tunnels were round, but the corridors square, it meant that there should be a narrow gap between the outer frame and the rock face. If they could get into that gap, they would be able to get anywhere in the complex.

'And the best of it is,' Joe went on, 'that we'll be able to see in through those ventilation grilles.'

Meg's face broke into a grin. Maybe – just maybe – in the three hours she had before her dad arrived, she would discover how the massive, trundling creatures had been brought back from extinction.

Arriving at the steel door, Joe switched off the beam of light. The tunnel was plunged into sudden – but not complete – darkness. All round the door frame, cracks of light could be seen, where the gap had been plugged up with rocks.

It didn't take Joe and Meg long to *un*plug it again. And five minutes later, the gap was wide enough for, first Meg, and then Joe, to squeeze themselves through.

The square corridor was smaller than the door frame, and once they had made it to the other side of the narrow opening, the tunnel widened out. Ahead of them, a fan of light shone on the curved wall of stone. It was the first of the ventilation grilles. They crouched down, peered in – and found themselves looking up and down an empty corridor. Joe rattled the grille.

'It seems pretty flimsy,' he said.

They walked on, stopping each time they came to another of the grilles. At first, they saw nothing but the same corridor. It was only when they came to a natural opening in the rock that things became more interesting.

The design of the complex had been largely based on the existing cave system. Wherever a natural cave occurred, so an internal laboratory had been built. They saw the inside of the rat and monkey laboratories and, after a long stretch of tunnel, came to the laboratory the professor had shown them. Unlike then, the room was now full.

A dozen women and men in white coats were hurrying about their work, filling racks of test-tubes, warming glass beakers over Bunsen burners and plunging flasks into vats of steaming liquid nitrogen.

'They seem to have stepped up production,' Joe whispered.

A woman close to the grille turned to the man

next to her. 'What was that?' she said. 'It sounded like whispering.'

Meg and Joe froze.

'It's the air conditioning system,' came the reply. 'You haven't worked in here before, have you? The wind whistles in the ducts.'

The woman was unconvinced. She strode towards the grille.

Heart thumping, Meg crawled off as quickly and quietly as she could. As the tips of the woman's fingers appeared in the grille, Meg realized that everything had changed. Up to this point, it had all been a wonderful adventure. Now she was doing something wrong, and if she got caught she'd be in big, big trouble.

'I'm telling you,' she heard the man saying. 'It's the air currents.' He laughed. 'The professor swears the place is haunted.'

The woman's fingers disappeared. 'Professor Wilhelm von Klett believes in ghosts?' she said, and burst out laughing. 'Now I've heard everything!'

Meg and Joe took the opportunity to slip away. They continued in silence. Through the ventilation grilles they saw more laboratories, more offices, more corridors.

'What exactly are we looking for?' said Joe some while later.

'Information,' said Meg. 'I want to find out as much as possible about . . .'

Abruptly, Joe silenced her with his finger on his lips. There were voices coming from up ahead. Meg and Joe crept forward. As they did so, the murmuring became more distinct.

There were three voices, all male. One was high-pitched, one was soft, and one was a booming baritone. Closer still, and Meg and Joe could make out words and phrases. '. . . uncontrollable . . . a law unto himself . . .' the high-pitched voice complained. '. . . an unacceptable breach of security . . .' boomed the second voice.

Next to the grille at last, Meg and Joe peeked in at the plush office on the other side. Two men sat at a desk. The third – the booming one – was standing by the door with his hands clasped behind his back. It was Mulligan.

'It's more than my job's worth to allow intruders,' he was saying.

'We understand, Mulligan,' trilled a plump individual with thinning hair. 'No one is holding you responsible. You may go now.'

'Sir,' said Mulligan crisply, and left the room.

The third man peered over his gold-rimmed

glasses. 'Right, Simkiss,' he said, his voice thin and cold. 'Now we've got all that sorted that out, I want to return to the matter of the professor.'

'At once, Mr Baker,' said Simkiss, opening the file that lay on his lap. 'Where would you like to start?'

'I think the beginning would be a good place,' came the icy reply. 'Don't you?'

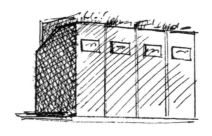

CHAPTER 15

Eavesdropping

Simkiss cleared his throat. 'Sir,' he said. 'With respect, it has been nine years since you last visited the institute. In all that time I have kept you informed of all the latest developments. It would be helpful if you could tell me which area you wish me to deal with now.'

Baker slammed his hand down on the desk. 'Kept me informed?' he said angrily. 'You *informed* me that the cloning programme was fully operational, yet I discover the value of the snow-leopard pelts had plummeted because they were all the same.'

'But, sir . . . ' Simkiss began.

'You *informed* me,' he went on, 'that the success rate of fertilized cells has been improving each year . . . '

'But it *has* improved,' Simkiss protested.

'It's still only one per cent!' Baker roared. 'One per cent! Do you not realize how big this project is? Even if there was a hundred per cent success rate, it still wouldn't be enough.'

Simkiss lowered his head, and began shuffling through the papers in his file. 'The . . . the snow leopard incident was unfortunate,' he said, his high-pitched voice cracking. 'Professor von Klett failed to inform me that all the clones had come from one donor animal. This, however, is now being . . .'

'Simkiss, Simkiss,' Baker said, his voice patronizing and nasal. 'You are still thinking too small. I did not set up a multi-billion complex in the middle of nowhere for the sake of a few fur coats.'

'Sir?' said Simkiss uncertainly.

'What you must grasp is this,' Baker continued. 'The good professor's work with cloning has given us a never-ending supply of natural products. Technology is at a turning point, Simkiss. Instead of trying to create newer and better man-made materials, we can return to the original – and best – materials. Animals.'

'But surely there will be problems,' Simkiss said. 'People don't like exploiting animals these days. There are animal rights groups, campaigners against the fur trade, the ivory trade . . .'

Baker snorted. 'Once people realize that there is a plentiful supply of whatever animal they need, they will forget all this nonsense about animals' rights. People will eat what they want, wear and hunt what they want, safe in the knowledge that animals are cheap and renewable, just like . . . like drink cans.'

Simkiss smiled weakly. 'You were right, sir,' he said. 'I hadn't fully understood the scale of the project.'

'Indeed, you hadn't,' said Baker. 'And I hope you now also understand the importance of Professor von Klett in all this. So, tell me. Can he still be trusted?'

Simkiss sighed, and crossed his hands in his lap. 'It's difficult to say, sir,' he said. 'As you know, the one condition the professor made when he signed up with Geo Exploration was that endangered species would be introduced back into the wild. I don't know how he would react if he discovered your plans for hunting them . . .'

'We had to think of something to do with all those useless snow leopards!' Baker smirked. 'I commissioned a little market research. You wouldn't believe how many rich people there are who would pay through the nose to go hunting. With a hunting group of twelve, we're looking at a quarter of a million per animal. With that sort of profit, the professor can fill the . . . the . . . Where do snow leopards come from?'

'The mountains of Central Asia,' Simkiss replied.

'Quite,' said Baker. 'He can fill the mountains of Central Asia with snow leopards. People will be glad of a few hunters to keep their numbers down!' he added, and laughed unpleasantly.

'The trouble is,' Simkiss continued, 'Professor

von Klett has become very difficult. A loose cannon. He has shown complete strangers around the institute. He has even threatened to tell the press about the mammoths . . .'

'He . . . ? Did you say *mammoths*?' Baker exclaimed.

'Yes, sir,' said Simkiss, puzzled by his boss's surprise. 'Three of them. I have been keeping you up to date with the progress.'

'Mammoths,' Baker said again, and shook his head. 'I knew he had cells from some extinct animal . . . But he told me it was some kind of rodent. The Siberian Giant Mouse, that was it.'

'Sir, the Giant Mouse *is* a mammoth,' Simkiss said. 'It's the name the locals gave to the creatures they kept digging up on the frozen plains of the tundra. They'd never heard of mammoths.' He sighed. 'I'm afraid the professor has tricked me. He told me that because the operation was so top secret, you and he had agreed that in all communication *Giant Mouse* should be used instead of *mammoth*.'

'And I thought they *were* mice,' said Baker. He chuckled. 'So the old buzzard has gone and produced mammoths. Well, well.' He leant forward and smirked. 'Think of how much a zoo or a game park would pay for one. And the ivory, Simkiss!' he said. 'This could be our best product yet!' His face grew serious. 'It makes it all the more important that we can trust the professor.'

'Or perhaps not,' Simkiss said softly. 'The breakthrough in the cloning process has been made. All the professor's information is stored on the central computer. Any number of top scientists could be brought in to work on his ideas. Professor von Klett is no longer necessary.'

'But . . . but we can't sack him,' said Baker. 'He'd run straight to the newspapers . . .'

'I wasn't suggesting that,' Simkiss said, his voice little more than a whisper. His eyes narrowed. 'Accidents do happen,' he said.

CHAPTER 16

The mammoth enclosure

As Meg learned more and more of the work at Geo Exploration, her worries about eavesdropping faded away. The research station was little more than a billionaire's battery farm: an evil place run by an evil man. What was more, the professor himself was in danger. Together, Meg and Joe headed back down the underground tunnels. They had to reach the professor before anyone else did.

At first, they drew a blank. Then their luck changed.

Meg sniffed the air. 'It smells like straw,' she

said. 'And listen.'

From further up the tunnel came the sound of snuffling and snorting. A pool of dim light poured from the next grille. They crept forwards and peered in. Meg gasped.

'Now that *is* an elephant,' said Joe.

Meg nodded. 'An Indian elephant,' she said. 'A female. But why?'

Joe shrugged. He stared at the massive grey beast as she swayed her giant head back and forward, over and over. Her left back leg was manacled and attached to the ground by a chain. She could move no more than three steps in any direction.

'Poor thing,' said Meg, tearfully. 'It's not right.'

At that moment, a muffled cry echoed from further along the tunnel. The elephant pricked up her ears and stamped her feet. The chain jangled and went taut. She raised her trunk and trumpeted.

'WAAAAA!'

Her cry was answered immediately by a chorus of muffled yet plaintive calls. 'Mmwnaaa! Mmwnaaa! Mmwnaaa!'

'*Those* are the mammoths,' said Meg excitedly. 'They must be next door.'

The elephant tugged at the chain furiously. At first, Meg thought that the cries were frightening her. But then she saw which way the elephant had moved. She wanted to be with the mammoths, not escape from them.

'Let's go and see them,' said Joe, and the two of them crept along the narrow gap to the next grille, where they crouched and looked in.

The three mammoths were inside a steel-barred pen. Two were standing, trumpeting forlornly. The third – still groggy from the tranquillizer – was lying on the straw.

'Look!' Joe gasped.

Meg had already seen. Crouching down next to the third mammoth, was Professor von Klett.

He was stroking the creature's head and talking softly. 'Can the three of you ever forgive me for what has happened?' he was saying. 'I did not create you so that you might remain locked up underground. I promise that I shall set you free as soon as I can. In deepest Siberia, where you belong.'

The two mammoths, lulled by his voice, walked up to the professor and extended their trunks. The professor held out his hands, and the mammoths blew on them.

'You'll see,' he went on. 'Mr Baker's a reasonable man. He'll agree to my proposals.'

Meg listened, horrified by the professor's misplaced trust. 'We've got to tell him what we heard,' she said.

'I know,' said Joe. 'But what if he doesn't believe us? What if . . . ?'

At that moment, a sudden fanfare of loud trumpeting cut him short. The mammoths stamped their giant feet nervously. The professor turned and craned his neck in the direction of the door.

'Mr B . . . Baker . . .' he stammered. He climbed to his feet. 'I was told that you were paying us a visit. I . . .'

Baker strode towards him. 'Professor,' he said, and smiled coldly. 'So, at last I get to see your Siberian Giant Mice.'

'I – I can explain . . .' the professor said nervously.

'I hope you can!' Baker snapped.

119

To the rescue

So, in effect,' Baker said, when the professor had finished his explanation. 'You lied to me.'

'No. Yes. I . . .' the professor blustered. 'I had to. If you'd come in person, I would have shown you everything. But I had to be careful. If the information had fallen into the wrong hands, the entire project could have been in danger.'

Baker nodded slowly. 'You were afraid someone might leak information to the media,' he said. His eyes narrowed. 'And yet I understand from Simkiss that you yourself were thinking of going to the press.'

The professor was taken aback. 'I . . . I might have said the press would be interested in my work,' he said. 'But I would never have contacted them myself. The mammoths are wild and noble creatures. I have given them a second chance at survival, to return to the land they left thousands of years ago – not to be treated as circus freaks.'

Baker nodded again, and turned to the mammoths. 'Fine tusks,' he commented. 'All that ivory . . .'

'NO!' shouted the professor. His eyes blazed. 'They are not to be killed for their ivory. I absolutely forbid it!'

Alarmed by the professor's raised voice, the mammoths started trumpeting again. The third mammoth climbed to its feet, and all three began stamping about dangerously.

'*You* forbid it?' Baker snorted. 'You overestimate your importance, Professor. We have all your scientific data on computer.' He smiled humourlessly. 'Essential, because you *might* be involved in an accident.'

'Accident?' the professor said quietly.

Baker nodded, and rattled the gate of the mammoth pen loudly. 'Accidents do happen,' he said.

Alarmed by the clattering noise, the mammoths grew more and more agitated. They shook their heads. They reared up on their back legs. They collided with one another and crashed against the barriers.

'Joe,' said Meg, tugging urgently at his sleeve. 'We've got to do something before the professor's trampled to death.'

Joe nodded grimly. He crouched down as best as he could in the narrow gap and silently pushed the length of tubing through one of the squares in the metal grating. Then he slid the tranquillizer dart into the end of the pipe. It was a tight fit.

At that moment, the professor cried out as one of the mammoths knocked into him. He tumbled down, out of sight.

'Hurry up!' said Meg urgently.

Joe ignored her. He knew that if he hurried, he would miss. He brought the pipe up to his lips and carefully took aim. Then he filled his

cheeks with air and – *pfwaa* – blew out with all his force.

For a terrible moment the dart did not move. Then, with a sudden explosion of air, it flew down the pipe, through the grille and embedded itself in the top of Baker's leg.

'*Yow*!' he cried out.

Designed for mammoths, the tranquillizer worked quickly on the man. Before his fingers closed round the small dart, Baker was already swooning. As he pulled it out, he staggered and passed out.

'Well done!' Meg exclaimed. 'Let's see if the professor's OK.'

'Stand back, then,' said Joe.

He raised his foot and kicked out savagely at the ventilation grille. There was a loud crack, the sound of splintering – and the grating clattered to the floor.

Meg dived through the hole and sped across to the mammoth pen. Joe followed close behind. They looked inside. Meg gasped.

The old man was lying on the straw in the middle of the pen. He was not moving. The mammoths – calmer now – were shuffling around him.

'Professor,' Meg called softly. She didn't want to panic the mammoths again. 'Professor von Klett. Can you hear me?'

As if waking from a deep sleep, the professor rolled over. His eyes snapped open and focused on Meg and Joe.

'You!' he exclaimed. 'But . . .'

'It's a long story,' said Meg.

'And we haven't got much time,' said Joe. 'Baker could wake up at any moment.'

'Wake up?' said the professor.

Meg grinned. 'Mr Baker had a bit of an accident with a tranquillizer dart,' she said.

The professor's eyes twinkled. 'So, he was right,' he said. 'Accidents *do* happen.'

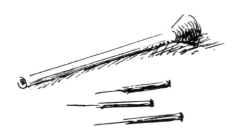

CHAPTER 18

Persuasion

After a brief medical examination, the professor announced that Mr Baker would remain asleep for some while longer. Meg glanced at her watch. It was nearly five o'clock. If Joe's calculations were correct, then her dad and the others would soon be arriving. She turned to the professor.

'What I don't understand,' she said, 'is where you got the cells to clone the mammoths from in the first place?'

'I was in the right place at the right time,' he explained. 'Twelve years ago, I was taking an internal flight across Siberia, when a storm struck. The pilot was forced to make an emergency landing. Thankfully, a group of nomads saw the plane coming down. If it hadn't been for them, we would all have died in the barren wilderness.'

Meg shuddered knowingly.

'I made my discovery on the fifth day there,' the professor went on. 'Bored with sitting round, I went out with a hunting party. I thought we were looking for an elk or a reindeer. Instead, we returned with a woolly mammoth.'

'But how?' said Joe. 'I thought they were all dead.'

'It *was* dead,' said the professor. 'It had become trapped in the boggy ground and died there over 10,000 years earlier. Yet it had been perfectly preserved in the ice-cold mud. It wasn't the only mammoth ever found – in fact the first recorded one was dug up back in 1806. But the tribesmen had no idea what they were.' He chuckled. 'They called them *Giant Mice*!'

'So did Baker,' said Meg quietly.

'Of course,' the professor continued, 'once

exposed to the air the mammoths quickly rot away. But when they are first dug up, the flesh is fresh enough to be eaten.'

'After 10,000 years!' Meg gasped. 'That's unbelievable!'

'Yet I saw it with my own eyes,' said the professor. 'Then I realized that if the creature was that well preserved, perhaps the DNA in individual cells might still be intact. I took a sample from the mammoth's belly, put it into my vacuum flask and packed it with ice.' He looked fondly at the three mammoths. 'The rest, as they say, is history.'

Meg frowned thoughtfully. 'And the elephant . . .' she began.

'Flossy provided the eggs into which I implanted the nuclei of the mammoth cells,' the professor explained. 'She gave birth to all three of the mammoths. Cleo, nine years ago. Minerva, seven years ago. And Boadicea, five years ago. I wanted to check their long-term development before cloning more.'

Meg looked at the three mammoths. 'As they're clones,' she said, 'maybe you should have called them Cleo, Cleo and Cleo.'

'Oh, no,' the professor said. 'They may be clones, but they each have their own personality. Cleo is a natural leader. Minerva, more of a follower. While little Boadicea is the boldest of them all. It proves that we are formed by a combination of our genetic make-up *and* our environment. Fascinating, don't you think?'

Meg nodded sadly. 'It's just such a pity that all your hard work has been for nothing.'

The professor spun round. 'What do you mean?' he said.

Meg nodded towards the still sleeping body of Mr Baker. 'You heard what he said, Professor,' she said. 'He doesn't need you now. He has all the information he needs.' She looked at the mammoths. 'And without *you* to protect them . . .'

'My babies!' the professor exclaimed. 'But what can I do?'

'There's only one thing you can do,' said Meg. 'You must tell the whole world about them.'

'Never!' he said angrily.

'Professor, the time for secrets is over,' said Meg. 'Behind closed doors, Baker can do what he wants. But if you go public, he won't dare harm you *or* the mammoths.'

The professor shook his head. 'Even if I did agree to go public,' he said, 'how would I go about it?'

Meg took a deep breath. It was time to tell the professor the *real* reason why she and her father had visited Bolam Island. This time she left nothing out.

'Ted Sundberg,' the professor said quietly. 'I've heard of him.'

'Like you, he believes that something must be done to stop creatures becoming extinct,' said Meg. 'He'd be all in favour of your work.'

'He would?' the professor said thoughtfully. 'The problem is, you see,' he said, 'that cloning and genetic engineering are so new that there are not enough laws to tell us what we can and cannot do.'

'Perhaps if they find out about Geo Exploration, then everyone will demand those laws,' said Meg.

The professor nodded gravely. 'What time did you say your dad was arriving?'

CHAPTER 19

In the can

Having helped drag Baker to a quiet corner of the mammoth quarters, the professor grabbed his coat and led the way back along the corridors to the heavy steel door that led outside. He opened it, and the three of them left.

'I hope Dad manages to find the place without that last bit of the map reference,' said Meg anxiously as they hurried along the tunnel.

'I hope they haven't already been and gone,' muttered Joe.

When they reached the cave entrance they both sighed with relief. In the distance were two bright beams of light. They were heading straight for them.

'Over here!' Meg yelled, and she and Joe jumped up and down and waved their arms about. The headlamps of the approaching snowmobiles flashed on and off. 'They've seen us,' said Meg. 'I'm going down to meet them.'

Five minutes later, Ted and Ricky drew up in one snowmobile; Nanuk and Donna in the other. They all jumped out.

'Meg!' her dad exclaimed, and gave her an enormous hug. 'You don't know how worried I've been!'

'I'm sorry, Dad, but . . .' She pulled away. 'We've got something *really* important to show you.'

As they made their way back to the cave Meg, Joe and the professor explained what had been going on. At first, Ted Sundberg could hardly believe what he was hearing.

'Let me get this straight,' said Ted Sundberg to the professor. 'You are running a cloning operation here. You have successfully cloned natterjack toads, snow leopards and . . . and *mammoths.'*

'It's true, Dad,' said Meg.

'And now you want me to film your work,' he went on.

The professor nodded sadly. 'It's the only way I can stop Baker,' he said.

The outer door was in sight when the air was suddenly torn apart by a wailing siren.

'Blast!' the professor exclaimed. 'I can't have shut that door properly. The alarm goes off automatically if it's left open for more than fifteen minutes. Wait here,' he said. 'I'll go and sort it out with the guards.'

As the professor hurried away, Ted Sundberg turned to his daughter. 'If what he says is true,' he said, 'then Professor von Klett is a remarkable man.'

'He's a genius,' said Meg simply.

The next moment the wailing siren became louder again as the door re-opened. The professor appeared. 'I've told the guards that it was a false alarm and they're trying to switch it off,' he shouted. 'Now follow me.'

* * *

In their pen, Cleo, Minerva and Boadicea were being driven crazy by the deafening siren. They tossed their heads, they stamped their feet, they lifted their trunks and trumpeted furiously – at the lights, at the noise, at the awful warmth of their prison.

'MMWNAAAAAAAA-OOO!!!' they bellowed, their cry a mixture of fury and despair as they battered against the bars of their pen.

Having tasted the great outdoors, they wanted to leave this underground prison and step outside – forever.

'MMWNAAAAAAAA-OOO!!!'

* * *

At the other end of the institute, the noise was causing problems of a different kind. Although Ted was getting some excellent footage of the laboratories, the wailing siren meant that he would have to add the sound track later. It was only when they arrived at the snow leopards that the siren finally cut out.

'Thank heavens for that!' said Ted, and

nodded to Donna to record. He turned to Professor von Klett. 'So where are we now?' he asked.

'This room contains cloned snow leopards,' he said. 'One hundred and sixteen at present.'

The camera zoomed in on the cats. The furry microphone recorded their plaintive mewing.

'I'll take you to the cloning laboratories now,' said the professor. 'It's where all the tricky work is . . . Oh, good grief!' he bellowed as the siren started up once more. 'Now what?'

Instantly, the corridor was filled with panicking men and women. No one knew what was going on. A guard spoke into his radio, and the next moment four of them were pounding along the corridor towards the professor and the others.

'Uh-oh,' said Meg.

But the guards ran straight past them.

'What's happening?' the professor called out.

'It's the mammoths . . .' the reply floated back.

Ted turned to Ricky. 'Keep the camera rolling,' he said. 'I don't want to miss a thing.'

They ran through the institute with the others. The sound of the rampaging mammoths grew louder. The professor pushed into a room that the mammoths had just passed through. The others followed him.

'Who are these people?' demanded a voice, and Simkiss emerged from behind a filing cabinet.

'They're filming the place,' said the professor. 'Surely Mr Baker told you. I thought he told you everything.'

'He does,' said Simkiss, flustered. 'That is . . .'

A guard appeared at the door. 'The men are ready with the tranquillizer guns,' he announced.

'No!' the professor shouted. 'A second shot of tranquillizer will kill them.'

'But they're smashing up the whole place!' Simkiss protested.

It was true. Above the wailing siren came the noise of banging and crashing as the mammoths destroyed everything in their way.

'They're heading for the computer room!' shouted Simkiss.

'Are they, now?' said the professor thoughtfully.

'They must be tranquillized,' said Simkiss. 'Before they can do any irreparable damage.'

The professor shrugged. 'If you want to explain their deaths to Mr Baker . . .'

'No, no,' said Simkiss hurriedly. 'But can't you do something?' he said. 'They *know* you. Can't you calm them down?'

'I'll see what I can do,' said the professor. 'But stop that infernal siren. Now.'

He turned away and strode down the corridor. Ted Sundberg and the others followed him – and the trail of destruction. The whole place was covered with splintered wood, twists of metal and shattered glass as the stampeding mammoths had smashed every chair, every table, every desk to smithereens.

When they arrived at the computer room the professor stepped cautiously through the broken doorway and looked round. Like everywhere else the marauding mammoths had been, the place had been reduced to rubble. Bare wires fizzed and sparked. The air smelt of burnt plastic.

Abruptly the siren stopped. The mammoths turned round to face him.

'Cleo. Minerva. Boadicea,' the professor chided lovingly. 'Whatever have you been up to?'

Simkiss re-appeared on the scene a moment later. His face was white. 'What's Mr Baker going to say?' he gasped.

The professor shrugged. 'Don't worry, Simkiss. I've got another copy of everything.'

'You have?' he said eagerly.

'Certainly,' the professor replied, and tapped the side of his head. 'Up here.'

Simkiss smiled weakly.

* * *

Half an hour later, Algernon P. Baker stirred. He sat up and looked round the mammoth pen blearily. He was blissfully unaware of the fact that, while he had been asleep, the institute had been filmed, Professor von Klett had been interviewed – and his dream of controlling animal production was in ruins. As he climbed shakily to his feet, the visitors were already leaving.

'Goodbye, Professor,' said Meg. 'Are you sure you won't come with us?'

'No, I'll be fine,' he said, and smiled. 'Now that the computer records have all been destroyed, I am suddenly important again. Besides,' he added, 'I must think of my babies. Perhaps one day I will be able to clone a mate for them.'

Ted Sundberg stepped forward, hand outstretched. 'It has been an honour, Professor,' he said. 'I'll be in touch soon, and . . . thank you.'

'If anyone is to be thanked,' said the professor, 'it is Meg and Joe. I shudder to think what might have happened without them.'

Meg looked down at the floor and shuffled about awkwardly.

'There is just one last thing,' said the professor seriously. 'I have given you extremely valuable information. Use it well, Ted Sundberg. Make a difference.'

CHAPTER 20

Anything is possible

On their arrival back in Prospect, Ted decided to start work on a documentary about the professor's work as soon as possible. By the following evening, he and Meg were back home. And five days later, after working day and night on the material – cutting, slicing, over-dubbing – Ted finished the film. It was broadcast immediately as a *This World* exclusive on Saturday night.

The programme had a massive and immediate impact. By the following morning, the incredible work carried out by Professor

Wilhelm von Klett was headline news all over the world. Scores of reporters travelled up to Bolam Island to check it out for themselves – only to find that both the professor and his mammoths had gone.

Meg, of course, was worried that Baker was involved in their disappearance. He, however, insisted that the professor had simply chosen to go – and no one could prove otherwise. Even Joe, who wrote to her, could shed no light on the matter.

Despite the missing evidence, urgent meetings were held at the highest level in every country to discuss cloning – and to make sure that science worked for the benefit of *all* the Earth's creatures.

Make a difference. That is what the professor had said. And that is exactly what Ted – with Meg's help – had managed to do. Yet despite all this, Meg was still disappointed that the story of the mammoths had ended in mystery.

Three months passed before this was to change. It was then that Ted Sundberg's other film about the Arctic Circle – the documentary on the Inuit way of life – was finally broadcast. Although it made less of a stir, the programme was highly praised, and the following morning Meg scoured all the newspapers for reviews. And it was while she was doing this that she stumbled across a couple of small, yet interesting articles. Both of them were about a weird cry – a weird trumpeting cry – which had been reported in deepest Siberia.

'That's it,' she whispered to herself happily. 'The professor must have done what he promised he'd do, and released the mammoths back into the wild where they came from.'

And as the professor's words came back to her, she remembered how he'd also promised to try and create mates for them. She smiled. If anyone could do it, Professor von Klett could. As he himself had said:

Anything is possible. Anything at all.

About the author

Fact and fiction are often thought of as opposites – like black and white, and hot and cold. For me, both as a reader and a writer, the most interesting novels are those where the line between fact and fiction is blurred.

Recently, I have been reading a lot of scientific articles about extinctions and cloning and global warming. I decided to mix all the facts together to tell a story about Meg and her Inuit friend, Joe. Of course, what happens in *Snowblind* is fiction.

Or is it?